KNOW
THE GAME

A &
CB

Produced for A & C Black by

Monkey Puzzle Media Ltd
Gissings Farm, Fressingfield
Suffolk IP21 5SH

Published in 2006 by

A & C Black Publishers Ltd
38 Soho Square, London W1D 3HB
www.acblack.com

Third edition 2006

Copyright © 2006, 2002, 1994
England Basketball

ISBN-10: 0 7136 7896 8
ISBN-13: 978 0 7136 7896 3

A CIP record for this book is available from the
British Library.

Note: While every effort has been made to ensure
that the content of this book is as technically accurate
and as sound as possible, neither the author nor the
publisher can accept responsibility for any injury or
loss sustained as a result of the use of this material.

A & C Black uses paper produced with elemental
chlorine-free pulp, harvested from managed
sustainable forests.

Acknowledgements
Cover and inside design by James Winrow for
Monkey Puzzle Media Ltd.
Cover photograph courtesy of Empics.
All inside photographs courtesy of Mansoor Ahmed
Photography.
Illustrations by Dave Saunders.

KNOW THE GAME is a registered trademark.

Printed and bound in China by C&C Offset Printing
Co. Ltd.

Note: Throughout the book players and officials are
referred to as 'he'. This should, of course, be taken
to mean 'he or she' where appropriate. Similarly, all
instructions are geared towards right-handed players
– left-handers should simply reverse these instructions.

CONTENTS

THE GAME

Basketball is a fast-moving, exciting game that can be played on indoor or outdoor courts. In a full game there are 5 players from each team on the court plus up to 7 substitutes, but people often practise with less (or more) players per team.

THE PLAYING COURT

Basketball courts are marked out on a flat, hard surface. Standard dimensions are 28m (91 ft 6 in) long and 15m (49 ft 3 in) wide.

The court is divided by a halfway line. The half of the court that contains the opposition basket is a team's 'front court'. The other half of the court, the team's defensive half, is its 'back court'.

THE BASKETS

The baskets consist of rings and nets, one at each end of the playing court. The rings are solid iron, 45cm (18 in) in diameter and orange. They are 3.05m (10 ft) up, and horizontal. Nets are usually white cord suspended from the rings. They slow the ball momentarily as it passes through.

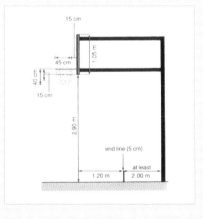

Here are the dimensions of the basket and support.

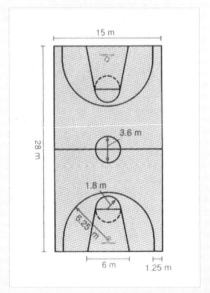

An international size court.

THE BACKBOARDS

The backboards measure 1.8m x 1.05m (6 ft x 3.5 ft). They are usually made of smooth, hard wood or a suitable transparent material 3cm (1.2 in) thick.

THE BALL

The ball is round and made of a rubber bladder covered with a case of leather, rubber or synthetic material. It must be between 74.9cm (29.5 in) and 78cm (30.7 in) in circumference, and weigh between 567g (20 oz) and 650g (23 oz).

For a match, the home team should provide at least one good, used ball. Neither team may use the match ball for warm-up.

CLOTHING

Basic playing clothing is shorts and a vest. Members of competitive teams wear identical kit, and must wear a number on their vest. The number on the front is 10cm (4 in) high and the one on the back 20cm (8 in) high. Numbers for international play range from 4 to 15. Numbers 20–25, 30–35, 40–45 and 50–55 can be used in some local competitions.

Basketball shoes can be either low cut or high cut. They need to fit well, and have a sole thick enough to cushion the strain of the jumping and landing that happens during a game.

BALL BOUNCE

When inflated and dropped on to a solid wooden floor from a height of about 1.8m (6 ft), the ball should rebound to a height of at least 1.2m (4 ft) and not more than 1.4m (4.7 ft), measured to the top of the ball.

WOMEN'S BALL

FIBA, basketball's international governing body, recommends a smaller 72.4cm (28.5 in) ball for use in women's basketball.

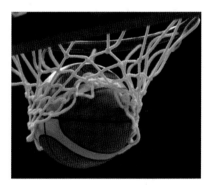

The net should 'catch' the ball momentarily as it passes through the basket.

Everyone can be involved, even when not on the playing court.

PLAYING THE GAME

The aims of each team are to score by throwing the ball into the opposition basket and to prevent the other team from scoring.

The game starts with a 'jump ball' (or 'tip off') at the centre. Once the ball is in play it can be passed, thrown, rolled, batted or dribbled in any direction. Both passing and dribbling are used to move the ball into a scoring position.

SCORING

Two or three points are awarded for a score from the field. Two points are won for shots taken from inside the marked semicircle 6.25m (20.5 ft) from the basket; outside it, three points are won. One point is awarded for a goal by a free throw (see page 49).

JUMP BALL

The jump ball is used to start play at the beginning of the game. One player from each team stands in the circle, on either side of the line across its middle. All other players must remain outside the circle until the ball has been touched by one of the jumpers.

The referee tosses the ball up between the two players, to a height greater than the players can reach by jumping. After the ball has reached its highest point the jumpers may tap it in any direction while it is on its downward flight. The jumpers may not leave their position until one of them has touched the ball. Neither of them may tap the ball more than twice. The player who has touched the ball twice may not touch it again until it has touched one of the other players, the basket or the backboard.

PLAYING TIME

The game is divided into four quarters of 10 minutes each, with a half-time interval of 15 minutes. The game watch is stopped when the whistle is blown, so no playing time is lost during stoppages.

The game is stopped when certain rules are infringed, and after a score during the last 2 minutes of play during the final quarter. The rules control four important aspects of play:

- contact
- progressing with the ball
- dribbling
- time rules.

A game cannot end in a draw. An extra period of 5 minutes is played, plus as many extra periods as are necessary to break the tie.

THE TEAMS

Competition games are played by two teams. Each team can consist of up to 12 players, with 5 players from each team on court at any time. The other players are substitutes and can be interchanged freely throughout the game, as long as the game watch is stopped.

POSSESSION ARROW

The 'possession arrow' is used to show which team gets possession at the next dead-ball situation. The scorer points the arrow at the team bench of the team that will next get possession. After a jump ball to start the match, this will be the team that lost the jump ball.

 Competing for a jump ball.

AIM OF THE GAME

The aim of basketball is to score more points (also known as baskets) than your opponents. Basketball allows all players to shoot, pass and dribble, so it is imperative that all players can perform these basic skills equally well.

INDIVIDUAL SKILLS

Basketball players need to develop certain playing skills within the rules of the game. Top players have learned several key skills to a high level of performance. These include:

- Passing and catching. Using either or both hands to catch, control, pass or shoot the ball. Players must not hit the ball with a clenched fist or deliberately play the ball with their foot.

- Dribbling. Players can dribble once each time they get the ball. The dribble ends when they touch the ball with both hands at once or allow it to rest in either or both hands. Having ended the dribble, players cannot begin another dribble until they have taken a shot, or the ball has been played by another player.

- If the ball was received while standing still, carrying it for one complete pace, but no more. If the ball is received on the run, a player may carry it for only one pace (i.e. a step with each foot) before passing or shooting.

Dribbling the ball past an opponent is one of basketball's key skills.

- Shooting and scoring from any point in the court.

- Movement without the ball.

- Footwork and pivoting. Once they have stopped moving, players are allowed to step once or more in any direction with one foot, while pivoting on the other. The pivot foot must stay on the floor at its point of contact, and players cannot change the foot on which they are pivoting. Sometimes the rules tell players which foot they must use as the pivot foot.

 Players should master controlling the ball at speed.

For example:

1 A player who receives the ball while standing still can pivot on either foot.

2 A player who catches the ball with one foot in the air can land on that foot to step. This foot is now the pivot foot.

LIFTING THE PIVOT FOOT

Players who get the ball while standing still, or come to a stop while holding the ball:

- May lift the pivot foot or jump when throwing for goal or passing, but the ball must leave their hands before one or both feet touch the floor again.

- May not lift the pivot foot when starting a dribble until the ball has bounced on the court surface.

At the end of the dribble the player uses his pivot foot to step past the defender to shoot.

Stride stop

To stride stop when receiving a pass, the player uses a full pace (one step with each foot) to stop. Having caught the ball when both feet are off the ground, the player lands on one foot and then steps forwards on the other.

The jump stop allows the player to catch the ball on the move, then choose their pivot foot after stopping.

STOPS

There are two methods used by players to stop when receiving a pass while moving or when finishing a dribble. These are a 'jump stop' and a 'stride stop'.

Jump stop

To jump stop when receiving a pass, the player takes the ball in the air, then stops by landing on both feet simultaneously.

When starting the dribble, the player's pivot foot remains in contact with the floor until the ball hits the floor.

PLAYING POSITIONS

Basketball is a game of maximum participation. Any player on either team can get the ball whenever it is in play, and players are not tied to any particular part of the court. Players can shoot from any position on the playing court. However, players do tend to specialize in particular styles of play and positions on the court.

DECIDING POSITION

The position players take depends on their skill, the skills of their team-mates, and the tactics the coach decides to use. Positional names – 'guard', for example – come from the area of the court usually taken up when the team is attacking. There are three basic court playing positions – guard, forward and centre (also called post).

GUARD

A player who plays in the guard position usually operates in the area of the court between the centre line and the opposition's free throw line, when the team is attacking. The guard brings the ball up court to start the team's attack, and is usually one of the smaller players on the team. Talented guards use their drive forwards to move in close to the basket – not necessarily for a shot, but to draw the defence in before passing to a team-mate in a better position for the shot.

FORWARD

Each team has forwards playing on the left and right sides. They usually attack in the area of the court between the restricted areas and the sidelines. The forwards will be among the taller players on the team, possess a good drive (see page 20) and be able to shoot well from the corner and side of the court.

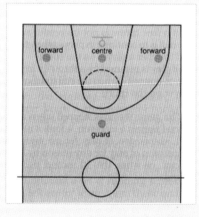

 Positional names with respect to the area of the court they cover.

CENTRE (OR POST)

The centre plays on attack close to the basket, and is expected to have the following skills:

- be a good shooter close to the basket (usually under pressure from close-marking opponents)

- have the ability to get free to receive a pass and remain close to the basket

- to take rebounds strongly.

TACTICS

The number of players that a team uses in each position can be varied, and depends on the tactics selected by the coach.

Players line up at the jump ball for the start of a game.

ADAPTABILITY

Basketball playing positions are not rigid: as a team's attacking play develops, a guard could find they are playing from a forward position, for example.

However, inexperienced players find it easier to understand their role in the team's attack if they learn to operate from these specific court positions.

The defenders in red mark particular areas of the court.

PLAYING ATTACK

Each player should consider themselves as an offensive threat, whether they have the ball or not. Standing and watching your team-mates does not commit your defender – this makes his or her job on defence a lot easier, allowing the defender to stay close to the basket and help their team-mates.

GETTING FREE TO RECEIVE A PASS

A successful pass involves two players – the passer and the receiver. If an attacking receiver is closely marked, he or she can aim to step across, putting their body between the defender and the ball. The aim is to place one foot in front of the defender's front foot, to force the defender behind them.

If the receiver is marked, a movement will be needed to lose the defender. This could be one or a combination of the following movements:

- towards the ball

- away from the ball and then back to receive the ball in the space created by the movement away

- towards the basket and then back to receive the ball

- a change of direction and a change of speed – in particular, changing speed from slow to fast (walk to run).

CATCHING THE BALL

Having moved free of their marker, players receiving the ball should:

- Make a target with their hands for the passer to aim at.
- Keep their eyes on the ball.
- Receive the ball by catching it in two hands with fingers spread, and cushion it by bending the arms.
- Try to get the ball under control in two hands as quickly as possible, so as to be ready to shoot, start a dribble or make a pass. This is usually called the 'triple-threat position'.

Attacking from a pass

Once the ball has been caught, attacking players should check if they are in scoring range. If there is no defender in line to the basket, the attacker could drive to the basket by using a dribble and a lay-up shot. If he or she is within scoring range and an opponent is not close, but is between the ball and basket, a set shot or a jump shot might be better.

SHOOTING TECHNIQUE

Players with a chance to shoot should follow these techniques to give themselves the best chance of scoring:

• Look for the shot early, concentrating on the ring before, during and after the shot.

• Hold the ball firmly in both hands, fingers spread, with the shooting hand behind and slightly under the ball, and with the fingers pointing up, wrist cocked back. The support hand should be at the ball's side.

• Shoot the ball upwards, with a full extension of the shooting arm in the direction of the basket.

• Flight the ball with a strong wrist and finger flick, following through in the direction of the shot.

• Be on balance and under control during the shot: this enables a smooth follow-through, which is essential for accuracy. Balance starts at the feet, so always establish a firm foot position, facing the basket, before shooting.

• Both the feet and the shoulders should face the basket on the release of the ball in a well-executed jump shot.

A player shooting at the top of his jump.

LAY-UP SHOT

The essential ingredients of the lay-up shot are that it is taken on the move, usually on the run. The player jumps up and towards the basket as he or she shoots, and stretches to release the ball as close to the basket as possible.

1 As the player moves forwards and picks the ball up at the end of a dribble or after receiving a pass, he takes the ball in two hands, lifting his head as he gathers the ball to check if the shot is on.

2 The player takes a long final step: a right-handed player lands first on their right foot and then on their left foot. This long step allows controlled forward momentum and prepares for the high jump off the left foot.

3 As the player jumps off one foot, he carries the ball upwards, still in both hands. The take-off foot for the shot should be opposite the shooting hand. The player releases the ball at full stretch from one hand, using the backboard to bank the ball into the basket.

The player reaches the top of his jump and extends his arm towards the basket.

Keep your eyes focused on the basket.

HOOK SHOT

A hook shot is useful when attacking close to the basket but with a defender close by and in a good position. This is similar to a lay-up shot except that players often start with their back to the basket, step so that their body is between the defender and the basket, and look over their shoulder to check the shot is on. The shooter jumps and takes the ball up in two hands, using a gentle flick of the wrist and fingers to make the basket.

SET SHOT

Although this shot has limited use in the modern game, it may be used for distance shots should the defender sag off. The set shot is also used for free throws, and it is useful for young players to develop this shot.

1 The player making the set shot takes up a 'stride' position with his feet, with the same foot forwards as the shooting hand. Prior to taking the shot the shooter bends his knees slightly.

2 The player looks at the basket throughout the shot. The movement starts with a powerful drive from the legs.

3 The shot finishes with the player at full stretch, following through with a vigorous snap of the wrist and fingers.

The ball should always be held in two hands prior to its release on a lay-up.

JUMP SHOT

This is perhaps the most effective shot in the modern game. It can follow on from a head or foot fake, a pivot, after receiving a pass, or at the end of a dribble.

1 The player aims to take off from both feet in a vertical direction. As he jumps, the ball is taken up in front of his face to a position above the head with the shooting hand behind the ball, just in front of the forehead.

2 The ball is released, near the top of the jump, with an upwards extension of the arm, and flipped towards the basket with a vigorous wrist and finger action.

DUNK SHOT

This is a shot in which a player jumps to put the ball down into the basket. It is similar to a lay-up shot except that the player reaches up with the ball to above the level of the ring (i.e. 3.05m/10 ft).

FOOTWORK

The stride and jump stops have been explained already (see page 11). The jump stop is particularly valuable in attack because after it has been made, either foot can be used to pivot. Players can use a pivot to establish balance, improve position and create space for a shot.

The ball is released at the highest point of the jump.

Stops and the use of pivot should be employed as part of a natural moving action, i.e. as part of a run or walk.

Some inexperienced players fall into the habit of bouncing the ball every time they receive a pass. This prevents another dribble and so limits individual attacking movements.

DRIBBLING

Dribbling is an essential skill because it enables players to move with the ball. Players control the ball by spreading their fingers comfortably, which allows them to contact as much of the ball as possible. The ball is pushed down firmly using hand, elbow and wrist. The dribbling hand should be on top of the ball. This prevents 'palming' (holding the ball) and ensures that the ball rebounds to hand accurately. Once players have mastered the touch of the dribble they must dribble by feel only, so that they can watch for movements by team-mates and opponents while dribbling.

Skilled players can dribble equally well with either hand, allowing them to change direction and speed. It is through these maneuvers that they can beat an opponent. Dribbling the ball towards the basket in an attempt to beat an opponent and take a shot is called a 'drive'.

 The dunk shot is one of the most spectacular moves in basketball.

THE DRIVE

The drive is used by an attacking player to beat a defender who makes a mistake. These are likely to be mistakes in balance and body position in relation to the attacking player and the basket. The main defensive mistakes that provide an opportunity to use the drive are:

- Moving towards the attacking player.

  This is the mistake most commonly made by beginners who, after the player they are marking has received a pass and is facing the basket, rush towards him. In this situation they can be caught off balance easily and beaten with a drive.

The fake and drive: the attacker makes a short, 'jab' step to the left and shows the ball in that direction, causing the defender to shift sideways in that direction.

- Jumping up to check an anticipated shot.

  While the defender is going up, the attacking player can drive round him or her for the basket.

- Moving backwards towards the basket.

  This gives the attacking player time and space for a shot.

- Sideways movement.

  If the defensive player is to the attacker's left, the drive can be made to the right, and vice versa.

FAKE AND DRIVE

A fake may cause the defender to make one of the above mistakes. For example, facing the goal and looking up towards the basket might fool the defender into thinking that a shot is about to be taken and to move accordingly. Sideways defensive movements can be triggered by a foot fake before the start of the dribble or, if the attacking player is already dribbling, by the use of a change of direction and a change-hands dribble.

A player in a stationary position facing a close-marking opponent is in a good position to use a fake and drive. For example, to move to the right of the opponent the attacker can step to the left with the left foot. As the defender moves to cover the fake, the attacker can step again with the left foot crossing over in front of the opponent, to step past and to drive to the basket. The player uses his right foot as the pivot foot throughout. The fake step should be a short 'jab' step.

> When starting a fake and drive, remember that the ball must leave your hand at the start of the dribble, before the pivot foot is lifted.

ATTACKING SIDES

If you are attacking, check which foot the defender has forwards. He or she will find it difficult to move the forward foot back quickly, so the attacking dribble past should be made on the side of the defender's forward foot.

▼ The attacker moves back to the right and starts the drive, dribbling through the channel opened by the defender's sideways movement. If the defender comes back sideways, he will probably give away a foul by creating contact with the attacker.

PASSING

To be effective a pass must be well timed, reaching the receiver when and where they want it. Getting this timing right is crucial to playing well. The receiver must get free to receive the pass (see page 14), and the passer must get the ball to them when they are free. An accurate pass will mean the receiver can immediately threaten to shoot, drive or pass.

Skilled passers try to disguise their intentions. They do not signal the pass by staring at the receiver or 'winding up' (telegraphing the pass with obvious body movements). Passes that are quick and firm, with a swift release of the ball, are often more likely to get to their target than a fast, hard pass. Fast passes require a preparatory wind-up, and give the opponents a chance to anticipate the pass.

CHEST PASS

This is the most important and basic pass of the game, used for fast, accurate passing at short range. From a position with the ball held in two hands at the chest, with the fingers alongside the ball and thumbs behind, pass the ball by fully extending the arms, snapping the wrists and pushing the ball with the fingers. Relax the elbows and extend the arms to follow through fully.

BOUNCE PASS

This is a useful pass to use for passing under a taller opponent or a player with their arms up. The pass is similar to the chest pass except that the ball starts from a lower position and is skidded by the passer to the receiver via the floor. The bounce pass can be made one- or two-handed.

When looking to pass, make sure you are aware of the changing positions of opponents and team-mates.

Your eyes should remain focused on the direction you want to pass the ball.

When a team-mate comes close to the ball handler, a short hand-off pass can be used. The ball is put into the air: the approaching player takes it as soon as possible after the ball leaves the passer's hand.

 The attacking player prepares to make a bounce pass.

TWO-HAND OVERHEAD PASS

This is a good pass for the taller player to use when passing over a smaller player. The ball is raised to a position above the head in two hands; from this position it is passed with a vigorous snap of the wrist and fingers directly to the receiver.

The ball is released with a snap of the wrist, even when passed overhead.

MOVEMENT

Once players have passed the ball they should look for opportunities to move to receive a return pass. One of the basic attacking moves in basketball is the 'Give and go'. A player 'gives' (passes the ball to a team-mate), then 'goes' (cuts to the basket looking for a return pass).

Defensive mistakes that will allow you to 'give and go' can be forced using a change of direction and pace.

This player is already looking to see where her pass could go.

GIVE AND GO

Any two players on court can work together in this way, but the give and go is most often used either between two guards or, more likely, between a guard and a forward. In this latter move the guard passes ahead to a forward and then cuts towards the basket looking for the return pass.

A player who passes ahead (as in a guard-to-forward move), may find that an inexperienced defender is tempted to turn to see where the ball has gone. At this moment the attacker is free and should immediately cut for the basket, signalling for the return pass. To make the immediate cut, a player needs to be well balanced, with knees flexed so as to be able to make the quick start that will make it possible to get past the opponent.

Having passed the ball forwards, this attacker can fake a sprint in one direction, before going past a defender on a different route to the basket.

The 'give and go' is the most frequent play in the game leading to lay-up shots and easy baskets.

 A player cuts into the basket to shoot.

 A competitive match at high/professional level.

PLAYING DEFENCE

Teams often win games by playing good defence. This restricts their opponents to poor shots from low percentage positions, or creates pressure on the attackers to turn the ball over to the defending team.

DEFENSIVE RESPONSIBILITIES

A player's responsibilities in defence against an opponent with the ball include the following:

- Discourage the opponent from shooting from a high-percentage scoring area.

- Anticipate individual opponents' moves so as to discourage them driving past for a shot from closer to the basket.

- Make it difficult for the opponent to pass accurately, particularly passes into the high-percentage scoring area.

When defending, try not to cross your feet – otherwise you will find rapid changes of direction difficult.

 Try to maintain a good defensive position: knees bent, head up, feet flat on the floor and about shoulder-width apart.

The defenders make a clean block on the shooter.

DEFENSIVE POSITIONING

To be able to defend, an individual usually takes a defensive position between the opponent and the basket. If the opponent is in a shooting position, the defender needs to be close enough to discourage the shot.

If the opponent is away from the ball, the defender can hang back a little distance towards the basket, changing stance to be able to see the opponent and the ball. In this position, the defender needs a stance with knees slightly flexed and head up, with weight on the balls of the feet spread approximately shoulder-width apart. This stance enables the defender to make quick movements, using a sliding action of the feet.

DEFENCE TIPS

- Good defence is not static: every time an attacking player moves, a defender should move; every time the ball moves, all the defenders should adjust their positions.
- Hands and arms play an important part in defence. They can be used to maintain balance and discourage offensive shooting, driving or passing.
- Good defence flows from the brain. Analyse your opponent's strengths and weaknesses, to reduce their scoring ability. For example, can your opponent only dribble successfully with one hand, or do they have a favourite shooting position? If so, you could adapt your position accordingly.
- If you realise your opponent is a potential pass receiver, change position and place a hand in the passing lane to discourage the pass.

ADAPTING YOUR DEFENSIVE POSITION

The basic defensive position when marking the ball handler is for the defender to stand between the attacker and the basket. When marking an opponent who does not have the ball, this position must be adjusted:

- Move into a position to be able to see both your opponent and the ball. It will help if you point one hand at the ball and the other at your opponent.

- Rather than positioning yourself directly between your opponent and the basket, move to a position nearer to the ball. This establishes a triangle of ball-defender-opponent. This position makes it easier to help cover if a team-mate is beaten by an opponent who dribbles or cuts towards the basket.

The player in red and blue (left) has established himself in a position where he can block his opponent's route to the basket, while gathering the rebound himself.

BLOCKING-OUT AND REBOUNDING

Competing for possession of the rebounds of missed, non-scoring shots is crucial in basketball. Players will try to get their body between their opponent and the basket, i.e. to 'block' the opponent out. This allows the inside player to have the best chance of gathering the rebound.

Red '4' starts to move towards the white attacker to block his path to the basket.

Rebounds for attackers

For the attacking team, gathered rebounds provide an opportunity for a second shot. If the player gathering is on attack he may try to tip the ball back into the basket. Should a tip-in be impossible, he should secure the rebound, land and immediately look to jump aggressively straight back up for a shot.

Rebounds for defenders

For defenders, gaining possession of the rebound gives them a chance to take the ball down court and mount an attack. If a defender gains the rebound, he or she will look to make a quick pass to a team-mate, or dribble out from the crowded under-basket area.

REBOUND SKILLS

These are the basic rules for blocking-out and gathering rebounds:

• When the shot goes up, make sure you know where your opponent is.
• Look for errors by your opponent, such as turning to watch the ball or getting too far 'under' the backboard.
• Step towards your opponent and pivot so that you are in position between the opponent and the backboard.
• Spread your legs wide with your knees bent.
• Touch your opponent with your back.
• Move with your opponent so as to block their path to the ball.
• Watch the flight of the ball and jump vigorously up towards it, using your arms to obtain extra lift.

Players who have not managed to block out their opponent have to compete for the ball in the air.

TEAM PLAY

In basketball teams will not win games if they only have one player who takes all the shots – they will be easy to defend against. Teams that have good spacing and inter-passing will create easy scoring opportunities for all their players on attack.

 Passing safely.

THE PERCENTAGE GAME

To achieve the basic aim of the game – scoring more points than the opposition – both teams play a 'percentage' game. This means:

- The team on attack tries to move the ball to a position from which they will have a high percentage chance of scoring.

- The defending team tries to stop the attackers gaining a position for a good shot, which limits the attackers to the poor percentage shots – the long range shots and those taken by closely marked players.

SAFE PASSING

Tackling is not permitted in basketball, so a team should find it relatively easy to retain possession of the ball. To do this they must:

- pass and catch with two hands

- use short-range passes (3–4m/10–15 ft)

- hold the ball ready ahead of the pass – this is usually at chest height or above

- discourage the use of long-range or lob passes

- ensure potential receivers of passes move free and signal to the passer

- have the passer aim to make accurate passes to the front of the receiver

- use fakes to disguise passing intentions.

SPREAD OUT

On the limited area of a court, the team on attack should endeavour to spread out so that there is 3–4m (10–15 ft) between each attacking player. This makes it difficult for one defender to mark two attackers, which in turn facilitates fast, accurate passes and gives space between defenders into which the attackers can move.

MOVEMENT AND CONTROL

The basic attacking play in basketball is a pass to a team-mate and a movement towards the basket, looking for a return pass. Beginners and inexperienced players frequently attempt to play the game too fast and make too much movement. Basketball is a game of changes of tempo: play may be built up slowly, then rapid movement is made as a scoring chance is developed.

Since there is no tackling in the game, emphasis should be placed on controlled movements about the court. A player should move only with their body and the ball under complete control.

Players around the halfway line, emphasising that an attack can begin slowly.

31

TEAM ATTACK

The attacking team aims to convert each possession of the ball into a high-percentage shot at basket. Attacking play is built on the skills of individual players working alone, but scoring opportunities usually come from two players working together. Occasionally scoring chances come from three attacking players working together.

Although some of the team plays that follow may seem complicated to complete beginners, they are relatively simple.

 Close-range shots are often fiercely contested.

Team tactics

To begin, each player in the team should follow these basic rules.

- Look ahead – face the basket you are attacking, particularly when you are holding the ball.

- Pass ahead.

- Move ahead – on getting possession, quickly start an attack by moving the ball ahead with a fast break, cut to the basket after a pass, drive to the basket, and get ahead of the team-mate holding the ball.

- Spread out – keep space between team-mates and leave the under-basket area clear.

- Position – most of the game is played without the ball, so move to help a team-mate, for example by making yourself open to a pass. Think before you move – where are you moving to, and what is your aim?

As soon as you get the ball, check your options: is it possible (in order) to shoot, drive, pass or move?

The start of a hook shot.

Drive and pass off

An attacking player who dribbles past an opponent may not be free to take a shot if a second defender moves across to mark. However, an opportunity has now been created to pass off to the team-mate who was being marked by the second defender. This highlights the need for attacking players to be alert and respond to the action of the ball handler, and be prepared to move into a good position to receive a pass (see 'Give and go', page 24).

Post play

Post play (also known as 'playing inside') is normally utilised by the posts or centres (see page 13) and involves offensive moves close to the basket. All players should be

Players contest the rebound of a missed shot.

able to conduct post moves, as players constantly interchange positions on attack.

Post play involves quick, strong pivots towards the basket to create close-in scoring positions. The starting position is often with the attacking player's back to the basket they are attacking: by making a quick pivot they will normally gain a position close in to the basket for a short-range shot such as a lay-up or hook shot (see page 17).

Screen play

The type of obstruction caused by the post player in the move above is legal. The obstructing of the movement of the defender is called 'screening' and is commonly used to free an attacking player.

If the ball handler still has the dribble to come, another team-mate (the screener) can move to stand with one foot either side of the imaginary line the defender would take if the ball handler dribbled to the basket. Once the screener is in position, the player with the ball drives close to the 'screen' (the team-mate). The team-mate is blocking the defender's route to the dribbler.

The dribbling player should now be free to move in for a shot. The screener must stay still if the drive occurs, but once the defender's movement has been checked, the screener moves to the basket, ready to receive a pass if one is made.

This screening action is often called a 'pick', with the movement of the screener called a 'roll'. The complete movement is referred to as a 'pick and roll'. If the defenders switch responsibilities, the screener moving to the basket will often be free to receive a pass and shoot.

In addition to the screen being set for the ball handler, it can also be set on a defender marking a player without the ball.

The screen play begins: the attacker on the right is receiving the ball, and still has his dribble to come.

Fast breaks can leave attackers with only one defender to beat – maybe even with none to beat, if they are really quick.

If you are moving forward with the ball down the centre channel to the basket, only pass off if your forward progress is blocked.

Fast break

The fast break should be an integral part of the attacking play of every team. In a fast break, the team on attack aims to obtain a numerical or positional advantage before its opponents can get their defence organised. The attack should start as soon as a team gets the ball. There should be an instant reaction to the change from being the defensive team to being on attack.

As soon as the defending team gains a rebound, an outlet pass from the under-basket area should be made. This first pass is often made to the side of the court. From here the ball should be passed or dribbled to the middle of the court. Once the ball is in the middle and moving down court, two team-mates should join the ball handler, creating a three-lane attack. The ball can be passed between these players, but as the attacking team moves the ball into the scoring area, the ball handler should be in the middle lane – this gives the opportunity of going all the way to the basket.

One player marking another very closely (to illustrate the injunction to 'pressure the ball').

TEAM DEFENCE

Any defensive tactic employed by a team needs to be based on sound individual defensive skills. An individual's defensive responsibilities are outlined on page 26.

When defending, a team aims to get possession of the ball without the opponents scoring, or to allow only low-percentage shots. To achieve this, the team will need to do the following two things:

• Defend the high-percentage scoring area.

This means that any ball handler on attack in this area must be pressured, to discourage a shot or to force a poor shot. If an opponent is within an area of court from which they would score a high percentage of any shots taken, then they should be closely marked to prevent pass reception.

• Pressure the ball.

The defence must try to take the initiative by attempting to pressure the opponents into errors. The ball handler should be marked, as should potential pass receivers.

Man-to-man defence
The simplest and easiest defensive strategy for a team to play is 'man-to-man' – where each defender is assigned to mark a specific opponent regardless of where he or she goes during an attack. Defenders concentrate on the opponent, rather than the ball. If the attacking opponent is a long way from the basket or the ball, a defender may 'sag' (move away from the opponent towards the basket being defended).

Zone defence
In a zone defence all five defenders work as a team unit and react to the location of the ball, rather than individual players. Each defender is responsible for an area of the court, and moves within this depending on

the movement of the ball. Players can be likened to a string puppet: if one defender moves then the remaining four defenders alter their position in accordance with the ball.

Matching attacking formation

The attacking team will try to dictate where space will occur, in particular by trying to draw defenders from the under-basket area. The defenders should match the formation taken by the attacking team, and aim to ensure that the under-basket area is defended.

Communication

Defenders must talk to each other so that they are all aware of attacking moves and defensive commitments. At the simplest level this will involve each player calling out the number of the player he or she is marking.

SWITCHING STYLES
Teams should not play a full game using only one kind of defence. They should switch between man-to-man and zone defence on a regular basis, so that their defensive form is not too predictable.

A player defending the 'under-basket' area. Defending the under-basket area will limit a team's high-percentage shots.

TRAINING AND PRACTISING

Good basketball players will not only need to master the skills and techniques of the game; they will also need to develop a level of physical fitness so that their bodies can cater for the sport's demands. Fitness training needs to increase as a player's ability improves.

COACHING SESSIONS

The club coach is responsible for planning and conducting training sessions. During these sessions the coach organises practices (called 'drills') to help club members learn new skills and develop their ability. Basketball drills involve repetition of the skill to be developed: these repetitive drills can also be practised by players on their own, away from the formal club session.

USE THE BALL

When training and practising for basketball it is important that the ball is used as much as possible in the session. The ball should be used not only in passing, shooting and dribbling, but also in defending against ball handlers and potential ball handlers.

▲ Only practice can prepare you for repeating the same shots again and again in competitive matches.

▶ Players from both teams practise shooting from different positions on the court prior to the tip off.

SHOOTING PRACTICE

A useful practice to employ is to start close to the basket, shoot and score. When you score, step one pace back from the basket and shoot again. If this shot scores, step back again; if it misses, step close to the basket and shoot again.

Start from a spot on the floor that you are fairly certain of scoring from. Vary the directions you step back from the basket after a shot.

With a partner, each take it in turns to shoot a set number of shots (e.g. 10, 20 or 25) and then change round. The shooter's partner collects the rebound and passes the ball to the shooter. The shot can be taken from the spot where the ball is received or following a short dribble.

Whatever shooting practice is employed, it is crucial that a high proportion of the shots taken score – practise scoring not missing.

Practise shooting from all areas of the court, inside and outside the 3-point line, and from all angles.

Practise shooting and scoring away from group training and matches, using a basketball ring fixed to a wall.

ONE-ON-ONE

'One-on-one' is a useful drill for practising individual offensive and defensive skills. One player takes the ball from a starting position about 4–6m (15–20 ft) from the basket, with the other player acting as a defender. The attacker tries to score using normal dribbling rules.

After each attack the players can change roles, or the attacking player may keep possession until he or she scores, in which case the attacker takes the ball back to the starting point to begin a new attack. Alternatively, each player may have a set number of attacks (e.g. 5 or 10), after which they swop over.

THREE-ON-THREE

'Three-on-three' (3v3) is a training activity that has become an established part of youth basketball.

Three-on-three is played in a half-court, into one basket. Each team has three players. The winning team is usually the first to reach 15 points, with at least a 2-point margin of victory, though this can vary, as can the duration of a game (which is usually 10 or 15 minutes).

One-on-one situations happen all the time during competitive matches, which is why playing one-on-one practice games is such a good idea.

In 3v3, try to fill each side of the court, to keep the defenders out and away from the basket.

Three-on-three rules

- The game starts from out-of-bounds with the team to take the first possession decided by a coin toss between the captains.

- Possession changes after each successful score, violation of the rules and defensive rebound. On the possession change the ball is 'taken back' to the top of the three-point arc and a new attack is started.

- Except for shooting fouls, fouls are penalised by the non-offending team taking the ball out-of-bounds at the side line, opposite the top of the three-point arc. Fouls on players in the act of shooting are handled as follows:

  1) If the shot is successful, one additional free throw is awarded to the shooter. Whether this free throw is made or missed, possession goes to the defence.

  2) If the basket is missed, one free throw only is awarded. If the free throw is scored, the ball goes to the defence; if it is missed, the ball is retained by the attacking team.

Practising one-on-one with a player who has different skills to your own will help you prepare for the same situation in a match.

WHY PLAY 3v3?

The three-on-three game gives the opportunity to develop many basic skills of the game, mainly because with only two other people on your team you get to play with the ball more. Skills include:

- Safe passing, since keeping possession is so important.

- Getting free to receive the ball – the passer needs a good target to hit with the pass.

- Good shot selection – a player should only take a shot when free and confident of being within range to score.

- Blocking-out and rebounding – rebounding a missed shot creates more possession of the ball.

- Playing good individual defence against a player with and without the ball.

- Making the basic team plays of drive and pass off, give and go, post play, and screen play.

SHUTTLE RUNS

Basketball requires quick bursts of speed over a relatively short distance, so shuttle runs should be included in a player's training regime.

The standard markings on the court can be used to measure the length of the shuttles. A player starts and finishes each shuttle at the end line.

- The first run is to touch the free throw line and back to the end line.
- Next run to the centre line and back.
- Next to the far free throw line and back.
- Finally, to the far end line and back to the finish.

Players should sprint at top speed throughout the shuttles. With rest periods in between, aim to complete two or three sets of shuttles during a training session.

FITNESS TRAINING

Basketball involves non-stop action and if players are to succeed they will need to be in good physical condition. Away from club training sessions, this could include running 5–6km (3–4 miles) two or three times each week to establish reasonable basic fitness. Swimming and cycling regularly will also increase leg strength and stamina.

REST AND RECOVERY

Players need to take care of their bodies by making sure they get rest when needed, and by eating and drinking healthily. Nutritional advice for young players is available from England Basketball.

Stretching is an essential part of preparation for practice and matches.

TIME RULES

Basketball is a fast moving, attacking game. To keep the game moving, its rules say that attacking teams have to perform certain actions within a given time. If they do not, possession of the ball is awarded to the other team.

You must take a shot or pass within 3 seconds of getting the ball in the restricted zone.

24 SECONDS

The team in control of the ball must make a try for the basket within 24 seconds of having gained control.

8 SECONDS

When a team gains control of the ball in its back court, it must get the ball into the front court within 8 seconds.

5 SECONDS

A 5-seconds time limit applies in three situations:

1 On a throw-in from out-of-bounds, the player making an inbound pass must throw, bounce or roll the ball to another player in the court within 5 seconds.

2 When a player has the ball for a free throw (see page 49), it must be taken within 5 seconds. The 5 seconds count starts when the ball is at the disposal of the player and finishes when he or she

releases the ball, or when the whistle is blown because the 5-second rule has been exceeded.

3 When any single player who is closely guarded is holding the ball and does not pass, shoot, bat, roll or dribble the ball within 5 seconds, this is a violation and the ball is awarded to the opposing team.

3 SECONDS

Players are not allowed to stay in the opposition's restricted area for more than 3 seconds while they or their team has the ball. This restriction stays in force for all out-of-bounds situations, but does not apply while the ball is in the air on a try for goal or during the rebound from the backboard.

> When playing close to your opponent's basket, remember to move from one side of the basket to the other, as this will avoid being caught by the referee.

BACK COURT

Players are not allowed to move the ball into their team's back court from the front court. This restriction applies to all situations, including:

- the throw-in from out-of bounds
- rebounds
- interceptions.

It does not apply, however, when a team has a throw-in from out of-bounds at the halfway line following a foul (see pages 46 and 49).

A player taking a free throw.

FOULS

A personal foul is a player foul that involves contact with an opponent. A technical foul is an infringement against the spirit of the rules, or the use of unsporting tactics to gain an unfair advantage.

The referee indicates to the player where on the arm contact occurred.

PERSONAL FOULS

If contact occurs in basketball, a personal foul can be awarded against the player the official considers to be mainly responsible for creating the contact.

Every player on court is entitled to occupy any part of the court not occupied by an opponent, provided that he or she does not cause any personal contact in obtaining that position.

The rules of basketball differentiate between a dribbler and a player who does not have the ball. A dribbler is expected to be in full control and be able to stop, change direction, pass or shoot in a split second. Dribblers should expect defenders to move into their path at any time, and should be prepared to take any action necessary to avoid contact.

Once dribblers get their head and shoulders past the opponent, the greater responsibility for contact remains with the defender. Contact by a dribbler on the chest of the defensive player will usually result in the foul being called on the dribbler. Should the contact be by the defender on the side of the dribbler, the foul should be called on the defensive player.

JUDGEMENT OF PERSONAL FOULS

The referee, having judged that illegal contact has occurred and blown the whistle, has to judge the severity of the foul.

- A 'normal personal foul' is a mistake by the player, an error in skill that caused the contact.

- An 'unsporting foul' is contact that happens when a player makes no effort to avoid contact, intentionally disregarding the ball and causing personal contact.
- A 'disqualifying foul' is a flagrant unsporting foul, e.g. a punch.

PENALTY FOR PERSONAL FOUL

When an official signals a personal foul, he or she indicates the player who has committed the foul. The official signals the number of the offender, the nature of the foul, and the penalty that is to follow to the scorer. This player's name and the foul are recorded on the score sheet. A player who has committed five fouls, personal or technical, must leave the court.

PLAYING THE BALL

The fact that a defensive player is attempting to play the ball does not justify making contact with the player in possession. If defensive players cause personal contact in an attempt to get at the ball from an unfavourable position, they will be penalised.

ADDITIONAL PENALTIES

Fouls are charged against the offender, plus the following additional penalties:

- Normal personal foul

  The non-offending team is given the ball for a throw-in from out-of-bounds at the sideline nearest the foul. However, once a team has committed four personal and/or technical fouls in a quarter, all that team's subsequent fouls are penalised by two free throws (unless the team committing the foul is in control of the ball, when the penalty is the same as before the four fouls).

 You should politely ask the referee what the call was.

47

ADDITIONAL PENALTIES (CONTINUED)

- Foul on a player in the act of shooting

  If the goal is made, it counts. Also, one free throw is awarded. If the goal is missed, two or three free throws shall be awarded, depending on where the shot was taken.

A referee explains his call to the player.

- Technical, unsportsmanlike and disqualifying fouls

  Two free throws are awarded to the opposition, except when a goal is scored by the fouled player (see page 49). After the free throws, whether successful or not, the ball is put into play at mid-court sideline by the free thrower's team. For a disqualifying foul the player must leave the game and playing area immediately.

PENALTY FOR A PLAYER TECHNICAL FOUL

Each offence is charged as a foul against the offender; two free throws and possession at half court go to the opponents. The captain designates the thrower. For persistent or flagrant infringements, players are disqualified.

TECHNICAL FOUL BY COACH OR SUBSTITUTE

The coach, assistant coach or substitute must stay within their team bench area. They must not enter the court without permission, leave their places to follow the action on the court, or disrespectfully address officials (including table officials) or opponents. A distinction is made between unintentional and deliberate infringements.

A coach may address the players, including substitutes, during a charged time-out (see page 51), and direct and encourage the team from the bench during the game.

PENALTY FOR A COACH/SUBSTITUTE TECHNICAL FOUL

Each offence by a coach, assistant coach or substitute is recorded and two free throws awarded to the opponents. After the free throws, the free thrower's team puts the ball into play at the halfway line. Persistent or flagrant infringements may cause the coach to be banished from the vicinity of the court, to be replaced by the assistant coach or the captain.

FREE THROWS

Free throws for personal fouls are awarded to the fouled player unless they are disqualified or injured. The thrower stands behind (not on) the free-throw line.

Nobody – even an official – can stand inside the free-throw lane when a player is taking a free throw. Other players can line up along the sides of the lane during a free throw, except following a technical foul or an unsporting or disqualifying foul. Two players of the defending team take the spaces nearest the basket, with the other players taking alternate positions.

The free thrower has a maximum of 5 seconds to shoot. Free throwers may not touch the line or the floor in the free-throw lane until the ball touches the ring or it is apparent that it will not touch it. Players lining up along the side of the free-throw lane can move across the line as soon as the ball is released.

The player is focused on the basket at the start of his free throw shot.

> When shooting free throws, always take a deep breath prior to beginning the shot. This should help to relax and clear the mind before focusing on the basket.

STOPPED PLAY

Play can be stopped for a number of reasons, including fouls (see pages 46 to 49 for more information about these). The clock also stops when the ball goes out of bounds or players commit a violation. A stopped clock allows substitutions and time-outs to be called.

Player waiting to come on as a substitute as another comes off.

SUBSTITUTIONS

Any or all of the five players in action can be replaced by substitutes during a game. The coach decides who gets substituted when, and makes substitutions in the following way:

1 The coach sends the substitute – who must be ready to play – to the scorer.

2 After reporting to the scorer, the substitute sits on the seat provided until the scorer sounds a signal. Then the player stands up and signals to the nearest floor official that he or she wishes to enter the court.

3 Once an official has beckoned the player on, the player comes on court immediately and the replaced player goes to sit on the bench.

When substitutions can be made

- Substitutions can only be made when the ball is 'dead' and the game watch has been stopped.

- Both teams can substitute when a foul or a violation is called. Substitutions when free throws have been awarded have to take place before the first throw is taken. The player taking the free throw can be substituted after the throws have been taken, as long as the request was made before the first throw. In this case, the opponents can also make one substitution.

Injury substitution

If a player is injured and in danger, the officials can stop the game immediately. Otherwise the officials wait until the play has been completed (i.e. the team in possession of the ball has thrown for goal, has withheld the ball from play, or the ball has become 'dead') before the game is stopped. If the injured player cannot continue to play, he or she should be substituted within 1 minute. If the injured player would have taken a free throw or jump ball, the substitute takes his or her place.

TIME-OUTS

A time-out is of up to 1 minute's duration and gives an opportunity for the coach to change tactics and give instructions to his players. Only the coach can request a time-out, by reporting to the scorer.

Each team is allowed to call two time-outs during the first half of playing time; three time-outs in the second half; and one in each extra period.

Teams can only call a time-out when the ball is 'dead' and the game clock is stopped, or following a field goal (goal scored during general play) scored by the opponents of the team that has made the request.

 Players huddled round a coach during a time-out.

OUT-OF-BOUNDS

The ball is 'out-of-bounds':

- When it touches a player who is out-of-bounds, i.e. a player touching the floor on or outside the boundary line.

- When it touches any other person, the floor or any object on or outside the boundary, or the supports or back of the backboard. It is considered to have been put out-of-bounds by the last player to touch it.

  An official shows which team is to put the ball back into play. The player throwing in must be standing out-of-bounds, behind the boundary line and near where the ball left the court. He or she throws, bounces or rolls it to another player within the court.

While the ball is being passed into the court, every other player must be completely inside the court boundaries.

When the ball is awarded out-of-bounds at the end line following a violation or infraction to the rules, the ball is thrown in from the nearest point to the infraction, but never from directly behind the backboard.

 This ball is out-of-bounds beneath the posts.

When an out-of-bounds ball is awarded to a team, an official must hand the ball to the player who is to put it in play.

HELD BALL

A 'held ball' may be declared:

- When two or more rival players of opposing teams have one or both hands firmly on the ball, so that neither of them can gain sole control without using 'undue roughness'.
- When the ball lodges in the basket supports. After calling a held ball, the referee checks with the scorer's table to see which team has the possession arrow pointing in their favour. The ball is then thrown in from the nearest point to the infringement.

 Players wait expectantly to start the game with a jump ball.

RESTARTING PLAY AFTER A SCORE

After a score, play is restarted by the opponents of the scoring team. One of their players throws the ball into court from behind the end line where the basket was scored.

CONTROL OF THE GAME

The officials in basketball are a referee and an umpire. They are assisted by a scorer, a timekeeper and, in top-class games, a shot clock operator.

Referees in the Euroleague are allowed to wear orange referee shirts.

OFFICIALS

The referee and umpire are required to wear a uniform of long black trousers, a grey shirt and black sports shoes. The referee and umpire jointly conduct the game according to the rules, and are responsible for imposing penalties for breaches of the rules and for unsporting conduct.

When play is stopped by one of the officials blowing a whistle, the official uses one of the standard signs to show the reason.

The referee is the senior official and is responsible for:

- the inspection and approval of all equipment
- tossing the ball at the centre to start play
- deciding whether a goal shall count if the officials disagree
- a team's forfeiture of a game when conditions warrant it
- deciding questions on which the timekeeper and scorer disagree
- examining the score sheet and approving the score at the end of each half

- making decisions on any points not covered by the rules.

A 24-second shot clock operator is required to operate the device for timing 24 seconds. However, when there is no such device this duty is undertaken by the referee or umpire.

REFEREEING TECHNIQUE

The basic responsibility of the officials is to have the game played with as little interference as possible on their part. It is the purpose of the rules to penalise a player who by reason of an illegal act has placed the opponents at a disadvantage. To be able to fulfil this responsibility a good official (referee or umpire) must:

- know the rules of the game
- be in the right place
- be looking at the right part of the court.

The officials use a number of hand signals to indicate their decisions to players, the table officials and spectators. These can be found in the official rulebook.

 The referee starts play with the ball toss at the centre.

 The referee should always hand the ball to a player and never throw it.

THE SCORER

The scorer's equipment consists of an official score sheet, a signal (horn or bell), five markers numbered 1–5 and two team-foul markers.

The scorer is required to:

- Record the names and numbers of all players taking part in a game.

- Keep a chronological running summary of the points scored by each team.

Substitutes wait on the sidelines to enter the game.

- Note all fouls and alert an official immediately when a player has committed a total of five fouls, or a team has committed a total of four fouls in a quarter.

- Indicate the number of fouls committed by each player by raising the appropriate numbered marker.

- Record the time-outs debited to each team.

- Sound the signal when a substitution or charged time-out is requested.

> The game watch is started when the ball touches a player on the court. It is stopped when an official signals a violation or foul.

 Table officiating is another way to participate in the game.

THE SCORE SHEET

The score sheet consists of three sheets: the original on white paper (this is for the organisers of the match); a copy on pink paper (for the winning team); a copy on gold paper (for the losing team).

When a foul (personal or technical) is called against a player, the scorer records this in the appropriate square against the players name, by inscribing a P for a personal foul, a U for an unsporting foul, a D for a disqualifying foul, and a T for a technical foul. In addition he or she will write a large X inside the box in the team fouls section for the player's team.

Time-outs for each team are also recorded on the score sheet.

THE TIMEKEEPER

The timekeeper's equipment consists of two stopwatches (a game watch and a time-out watch), and a signal (gong, horn or bell), which is different from the scorer's signal.

The timekeeper is required to:

- record playing time
- time stoppages
- indicate the end of playing time in each half or extra period by sounding the signal.

VARIATIONS OF THE GAME

Basketball is played in different forms by people with different abilities. The different variations of the game include wheelchair basketball and versions of the game for younger players.

WHEELCHAIR BASKETBALL

Wheelchair basketball is played by competitors in wheelchairs under the same rules (with a few simple adaptations), with the same ball and in the same court as the conventional game.

Wheelchair basketball players must be able to sit in and self-propel a wheelchair. Wheelchair basketball is played by people from almost all disability groups, including those with polio and cerebral palsy, amputees, paraplegics, and people with minor mental disabilities. Wheelchair basketball is the only team game in which nearly all physically disabled people can take part and compete on equal terms.

The main differences in the rules concern dribbling, progressing with the ball, and the 5-seconds restriction.

Jump ball

A jump ball is only used at the start of each half. Players remain seated, but stretch for the ball. In other held-ball situations teams alternate taking possession of the ball for a throw-in from out-of-bounds.

Dribbling in a wheelchair occurs when a player:

- Propels the chair and bounces the ball simultaneously.

- Alternately propels the chair and bounces the ball. The ball is placed on the lap (not between the knees) while pushing the chair, and one or two pushes must be followed by one or more bounces.

Any player can use these techniques.

A player in a wheelchair may progress with the ball in any direction within the following limits:

- The number of pushes on the wheels while holding the ball must not exceed two.

- Any pivot movements are part of the dribble, and are limited to two consecutive pushes without bouncing the ball.

3-second rule

Instead of the 3-second rule of the running game, in the wheelchair variation the restriction is 5 seconds.

MINI BASKETBALL

Mini basketball is a game for the primary school age group, based on the conventional game. The ring is placed 2.60m/8.53 ft rather than 3.05m/10 ft above the floor, and the ball is smaller than a normal basketball – approximately a size 5 soccer ball. Other differences are:

- A game is divided into four playing periods of 10 minutes. Each member of the team must play at least one 10-minute period, and no player can play in all of the first three quarters.

- There is no 24-second rule, three-point rule, or team-foul rule; nor are there time-outs, or bonus free throws after a basket is scored when the player is fouled in the act of shooting.

ENGLAND BASKETBALL

England Basketball supplies rule books, coaching manuals and a variety of other basketball resources:

England Basketball
First Floor
EIS – Sheffield
Coleridge Road
Sheffield
S9 5DA

Tel: 0870 774 225

www.englandbasketball.co.uk

 A young girl dribbles the ball over the court.

GLOSSARY

Assist A pass to an open team-mate that results in an immediate score.

Back court The half of the court that contains a team's defensive basket.

Bank shot A shot in which the ball rebounds from the backboard to the basket.

Blocking Personal contact which impedes the progress of an opponent who is not in possession of the ball.

Blocking out (boxing out; cutting out) The positioning of a player in such a manner as to prevent an opposing player from moving to the basket to gain a rebound.

Break The rapid movement of a player to a space where they hope to receive a pass.

Combination defence A team defence where some of the team members play to zone defence principles and others play one-on-one defence.

Controlling the boards Gaining the majority of the rebounds.

Cut A quick movement by an attacking player without the ball to gain an advantage over the defence, usually directed towards the basket.

Dead Attacking players who have used their dribble.

Double team When two defensive players mark one opponent with the ball, usually a temporary measure.

Drill A repetitive practice.

Drive The movement of an attacking player dribbling towards the basket in an attempt to score.

Dunk A shot in which a jumping player puts the ball down into the opponent's basket from above.

Fake A movement made with the aim of deceiving an opponent.

Fast break A fast attack that attempts to advance the ball to the front court before the defence is organised, with the object of achieving numerical superiority or position to give a good shot.

Feed To pass the ball to a team-mate.

Free ball (loose ball) A ball that although in play is not in the possession of either team.

Freezing the ball The action of the team in possession of the ball who try to keep possession without attempting to score.

Front court The half of the court that contains the basket that a team is attacking.

Give and go An attacking move in which a player passes the ball to a team–mate and cuts towards the basket for a return pass.

Hustle A characteristic of a player who plays hard at all times, especially when on defence. A player who pressures the opponent.

One-to-one defence A style of defence where each player is assigned to guard a specific opponent regardless of where they go in the attack.

Passing game An attack with the emphasis on passing the ball, with little or no use of the dribble.

Pattern play Attacking plays starting from fixed and predetermined court positions.

Play A term used to describe a series of movements of players and/or the ball on court, mainly used for attacking manoeuvres.

Playmaker A player who is adept at setting up situations that enable team–mates to have scoring opportunities.

Press A defensive attempt to force the attacking team into making some kind of error and thus lose possession of the ball. The press can be applied full court, half court or any other fractional part of the playing area and can be based on either man–to–man or zone (see below) principles.

Rebound A term used to describe the retrieving of the ball as it rebounds from the backboard or the ring after an unsuccessful shot.

Restraining circle The circles with 3.6m (12 ft) diameter located in the centre of the court and at the free-throw lines.

Screen A screen occurs when an attacking player attempts to prevent a defender from reaching a desired position or maintaining their defensive position.

Scrimmage A practice game.

Series A name given to a sequence of plays used by an attacking team in particular situations.

Set play (i) A repetitive, pre–arranged form of attack.
(ii) A play executed to predetermined and rehearsed moves which, when applied at certain set situations in the game, is intended to result in a favourable scoring chance. The set situations are usually out–of–bounds, jump ball or the free–throw situation.

Steal To take the ball from an opponent or intercept a pass.

Switch A defensive manoeuvre in which two defenders exchange defensive responsibilities by changing the player they are guarding.

System A team's basic attacking and defensive play.

Tip–off The centre jump ball at the start of play.

Turnover The loss of ball possession without a shot being taken.

Zone defence A team's defensive tactic in which the five defensive players protect an area surrounding their basket within normal shooting range.

INDEX